# Contents

# 1: The Threat of Global Warming

Global warming is a hot topic. You have probably heard the term in the news, read it in the newspapers and listened to politicians and environmentalists discuss it. But what exactly is global warming? Very simply, it is an increase in the average temperature of the Earth's atmosphere. It's a real threat to the Earth, to us and to the animals and plants that share our planet.

## What's causing global warming?

Most scientists agree that global warming is happening and that it's being driven by human activities – mainly the burning of fossil fuels (coal, oil and gas), which is adding millions of tonnes of carbon dioxide to the atmosphere every day. Changing land use, such as deforestation and cattle ranching, is adding to the problem.

## What's the problem?

We are already witnessing the effects of global warming. The Earth's atmosphere is warming, which is beginning to alter the climates (weather patterns) we are used to (this is why global warming is also known as climate change – the terms are used interchangeably). Side effects of the warming include melting glaciers and sea ice, rising sea levels and warming oceans.

In the future, global warming may cause substantial changes to the world we know, with more severe weather, changing coastlines and changing patterns of vegetation and animal habitats. How bad things will get in the long term is hard to say, but if we carry on pumping carbon dioxide into the atmosphere as we are, the effects will be catastrophic for millions of people.

## What's the answer?

The answer is obvious. We have to try to stop, then reverse, global warming, or suffer the consequences. But that is much easier said than done. It requires a radical cut in emissions of carbon dioxide, and that means equally radical changes to our lifestyles and to how we source the energy we need. That's not going to happen overnight, and even if it did, things would still get worse before they got better.

It's taken a long time for most of us to wake up to the problem of global warming. Some people (the global warming sceptics, many of whom are scientists) still do not believe it's actually happening, and if they do, they don't think it's a human-made problem. But most scientists do believe it. And they also believe that global warming is a serious threat to our planet, and one of our own making.

Global warming is likely to make coastal flooding more frequent. This aerial view shows flooded streets and houses on France's Atlantic coast after a powerful storm drove huge waves ashore. Fifty people died in the flood, and hundreds of homes were damaged.

# 2: Earth's Greenhouse

The air that we breathe, and that we feel when the wind blows, makes up a layer that surrounds the Earth, known as the atmosphere. The atmosphere is responsible for trapping the heat that causes global warming. So what's in the atmosphere, and how exactly does it trap heat?

## Layers and gases

The properties of the air in the atmosphere change with altitude. The air is most dense next to the Earth's surface. The higher up you go, the thinner it gets, until it fades away into space several hundred kilometres above the surface. Meteorologists separate the atmosphere into different layers. For our discussion of global warming, the bottom layer, called the troposphere, is most important.

The air in the troposphere is a mixture of many different gases. They are nitrogen (which makes up 78 per cent of the troposphere), oxygen (21 per cent) and other gases, including carbon dioxide, neon and argon (1 per cent). There is normally some water vapour in the air, too.

## The greenhouse effect

The process by which the Earth's atmosphere traps heat from the Sun is called the greenhouse effect. The Sun gives off visible light, infrared light and ultraviolet light. These are all forms of energy. When this energy arrives at the Earth, about 30 per cent is reflected back into space by clouds and dust in the atmosphere, and by the surface. About 20 per cent is absorbed into the atmosphere by water vapour. The rest (about half) is absorbed by the Earth's surface, into rocks, soil, plants and water.

## FACTS and FIGURES

### THE SUN'S ENERGY

The Sun gives out energy in the form of heat, light and other forms of radiation (such as ultraviolet radiation). It produces a staggering 400 million, billion, billion joules of energy every second, which spreads into space. About half a billionth of this energy hits the Earth. The heating effect is greatest around the equator, where the Sun's rays hit the surface straight on, rather than with a glancing blow (as happens towards the poles).

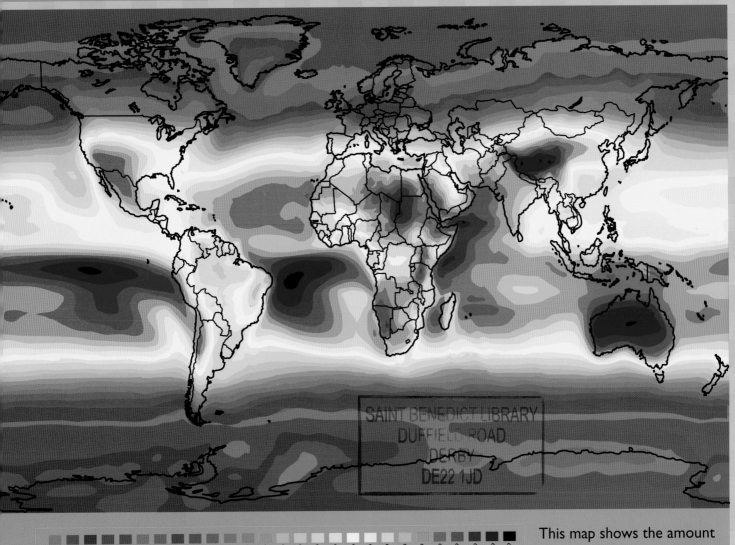

0 – 30  30 – 40  40 – 50  50 – 60  60 – 70  70 – 80  80 – 90  90 – 100  100 – 110  110 – 120  120 – 130  130 – 140  140 – 150  150 – 160  160 – 170  170 – 180  180 – 190  190 – 200  200 – 210  210 – 220  220 – 230  230 – 240  240 – 250  250 – 260  260 – 270  270 – 280  280 – 290

Yearly average of solar energy in watts per square metre

This map shows the amount of solar energy that hits different parts of the Earth.

But that's not the end of the story. The Earth's surface and some of the gases in the atmosphere emit some of the energy they have absorbed. Some of this energy is absorbed by gases in the atmosphere and then emitted again. As a result, as much heat is emitted into space from the Earth as reaches the Earth from the Sun. Critically, however, some of this heat is trapped temporarily in the atmosphere, making the atmosphere warm. It's similar to the way glass traps heat in a greenhouse – hence the 'greenhouse effect'.

Today, the average temperature at the Earth's surface is 14.5°C. Without the greenhouse effect it would be more like -18°C (but much warmer by day and much colder by night) and it would be impossible for life to exist on our planet.

## Greenhouse gases

Not all the gases in the Earth's atmosphere contribute to the greenhouse effect. The two gases that make up the vast majority of the atmosphere – nitrogen and oxygen – do not absorb heat at all. The main ones that do absorb heat are carbon dioxide, methane, water vapour and ozone. Because these gases are responsible for the greenhouse effect, they have become known as greenhouse gases.

The amount of each greenhouse gas in the atmosphere is very small, so the concentration of these gases is measured as parts per million (ppm). This is how many molecules of the particular gas there are in every million molecules in the air.

## Carbon dioxide

Carbon dioxide ($CO_2$) traps most of the heat in the atmosphere. Its current concentration is 380 ppm, and overall there are about 3,000 gigatonnes (billion tonnes) in the atmosphere. Carbon dioxide is found naturally in the atmosphere. Plants need it for photosynthesis and animals breathe it out as a waste product. It is also released into the air when wood or other natural materials burn, and when plants rot. These processes are all part of the carbon cycle – the constant movement of carbon between the atmosphere and plants and animals.

## Methane

The concentration of methane ($CH_4$) in the atmosphere is just 2 ppm. However, methane is about 20 times more efficient than carbon dioxide at trapping heat. Methane is released when plants rot slowly underwater. It is also emitted by cattle.

## Water vapour

There is always some water vapour in the air. The concentration of water vapour can be as high as 40,000 ppm (that's 4 per cent). Water vapour is formed when water evaporates from oceans and other bodies of water, and from the land and plants. It condenses in the air to form water droplets or ice crystals that make up clouds.

## Ozone

Ozone is a form of oxygen. The concentration of ozone in the atmosphere is about 35 ppm. Of all the greenhouse gases, it has the smallest effect. Ozone in the troposphere is made when sunlight interacts with pollution in the atmosphere.

## Reducing heat

Some substances in the atmosphere actually reduce the amount of heat that's trapped by reflecting sunlight into space. They include some types of clouds, volcanic ash and aerosols (which are pollutants). A giant volcanic eruption can reduce the temperature of the whole Earth for months, or even years.

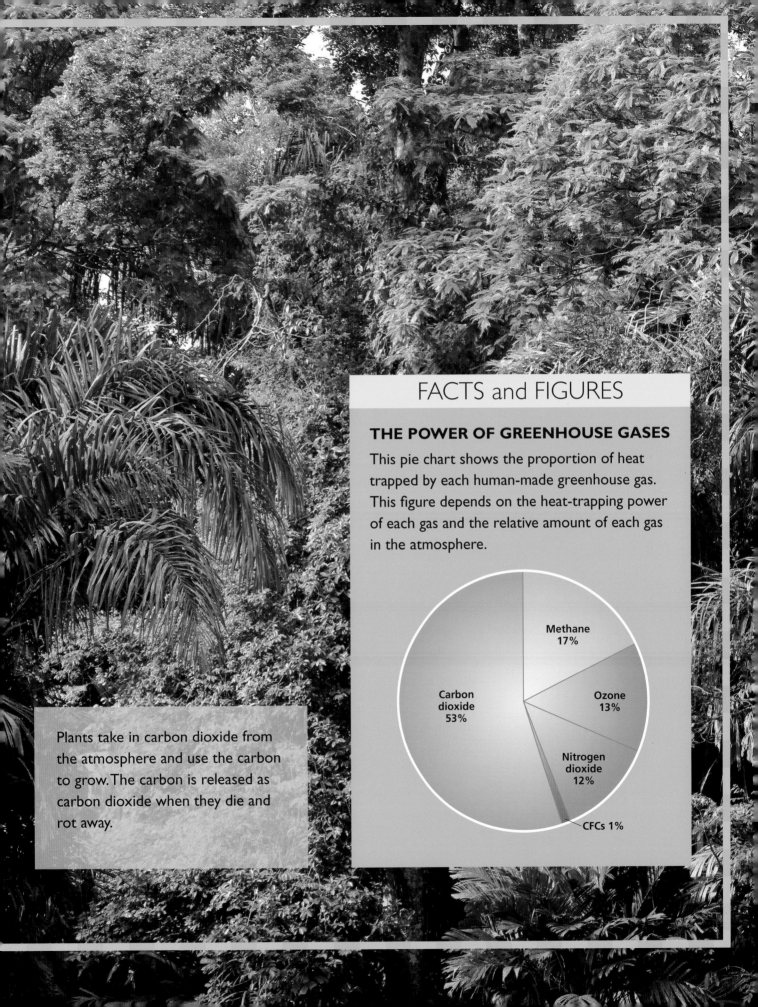

## FACTS and FIGURES

### THE POWER OF GREENHOUSE GASES

This pie chart shows the proportion of heat trapped by each human-made greenhouse gas. This figure depends on the heat-trapping power of each gas and the relative amount of each gas in the atmosphere.

Methane 17%

Ozone 13%

Carbon dioxide 53%

Nitrogen dioxide 12%

CFCs 1%

Plants take in carbon dioxide from the atmosphere and use the carbon to grow. The carbon is released as carbon dioxide when they die and rot away.

# 3: Causes of Global Warming

The greenhouse effect is a natural process that keeps the Earth warm. Global warming is the increase we are experiencing in the average temperature of the Earth's atmosphere. The temperature is rising because the greenhouse effect is stronger than it used to be, so that the atmosphere is trapping more of the Sun's energy than before. So what's causing it?

## More greenhouse gases

Most scientists agree that the greenhouse effect is becoming stronger because we are adding greenhouse gases to the atmosphere. The greater the concentration of these gases, the more heat is trapped. The more heat energy there is in the atmosphere, the higher the average air temperature.

## PERSPECTIVES

### DAVID CHARLES KEELING

Keeling was an American oceanographer who, in 1958, started making accurate measurements of carbon dioxide levels in the atmosphere. He showed that carbon dioxide levels were rising year on year. Keeling said the rise was:

*a real phenomenon. It is possible that this is merely a reflection of natural events like previous peaks in the rate, but it is also possible that it is the beginning of a natural process unprecedented in the [climate] record.*

Today, a line curving upwards on a graph that shows rising carbon dioxide levels over time is known as a Keeling Curve.

## Changing carbon dioxide levels

Carbon dioxide is the chief greenhouse gas, responsible for more than half of the greenhouse effect. In the 1750s, before the Industrial Revolution began, the concentration of carbon dioxide in the atmosphere was about 280 ppm. A century ago it had risen to 300 ppm. Today it is 380 ppm. Where has all this carbon dioxide come from? The main culprit is fossil fuels. Changing land use, including the destruction of the rainforests, has also made a significant contribution (see page 15). As carbon dioxide levels have risen in the last 250 years, so has the average air temperature across the globe. During the

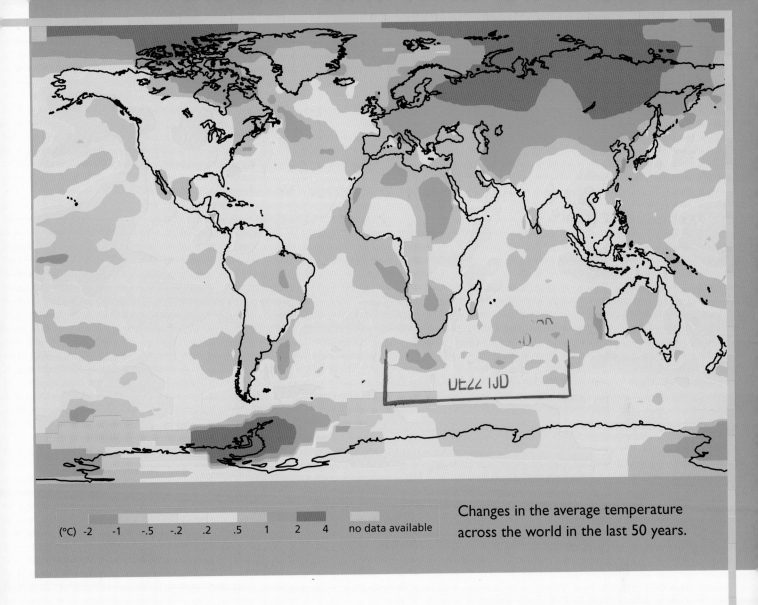

(°C) -2    -1    -.5    -.2    .2    .5    1    2    4    no data available

**Changes in the average temperature across the world in the last 50 years.**

last century the average temperature rose by 0.8°C. The map on this page shows that it has risen more in some areas, and fallen a little in others.

## Feedbacks

The atmosphere is a very complex system. It interacts with the oceans and land, exchanging heat and gases with them. As the temperature of the atmosphere (and the oceans) rises, other things begin to happen that influence the greenhouse effect. These are called feedbacks. Some feedbacks are positive, which means they accelerate the greenhouse effect; others are negative, which means they reduce the greenhouse effect.

For example, ice at the Earth's poles is good at reflecting the Sun's heat back into space. But as the ice begins to melt because of global warming, the exposed land and sea absorb more energy, accelerating the greenhouse effect. This is a positive feedback.

## Carbon dioxide from burning

The main source of the extra carbon dioxide we are adding to the atmosphere is fossil fuels – coal, oil and gas. They are called fossil fuels because they formed from the remains of plants and animals that died millions of years ago. Carbon dioxide comes from burning fossil fuels in electricity-generating stations, for heating homes, offices, schools and other buildings, and in road vehicle, aircraft and ship engines.

Because fossil fuels were formed from organic materials, they are made up of chemicals that contain the element carbon. For example, natural gas is mainly methane, which is made up of carbon and hydrogen. When fossil fuels burn, the carbon combines with oxygen to form carbon dioxide, which is a gas. This is released into the air. We don't notice carbon dioxide being produced when fuels burn because it is

Coal-fired power stations are major emitters of carbon dioxide, and there are around 50,000 of them currently operating around the world.

colourless and odourless. Water vapour, another greenhouse gas, is also produced by burning fuels. You can see this on a cold day as the water vapour in car exhaust gases condenses into small droplets.

When we burn fossil fuels, we are releasing carbon (contained in carbon dioxide) that was captured from the atmosphere by plants millions of years ago. However, we are releasing it far more quickly than it was captured.

## Carbon dioxide from rainforests

The world's rainforests are being destroyed at an alarming rate. They are being cleared by forestry companies for their valuable wood, by local farmers in order to grow crops, and by cattle ranchers to make space for cattle to graze. Like fossil fuels, plants contain carbon. As the forest trees and other plants are burned or rot away, carbon dioxide is released into the atmosphere. Because the forest cannot regrow, the carbon dioxide stays in the atmosphere.

## Carbon sinks

Only about half of the carbon dioxide that we put into the atmosphere stays there. The other half either dissolves in the oceans or is taken in by plants as they photosynthesize. The oceans and rainforests are known as carbon sinks. Without them, the concentration of carbon dioxide in the atmosphere would be even higher than it is. However, carbon sinks may not carry on working forever, and the carbon dioxide in the oceans could cause other problems (see page 34).

(see page 34)

## CASE STUDY

### SLASH-AND-BURN FARMING

Dense rainforest is no good for farming, so farmers cut it down to make space for growing crops or raising cattle. After cutting down the trees, they keep the wood, and burn what's left. This is known as slash and burn. After a season of growing crops or grass, the land is abandoned because the nutrients in the soil have been used up. Carbon dioxide from the burning goes into the atmosphere. The forest, with its soil depleted of nutrients, never recovers.

Huge numbers of cattle are kept on vast cattle ranches. They are the main source of the methane that is contributing to global warming.

## Personal carbon footprints

Any carbon dioxide that we put into the atmosphere is known as a carbon emission. The amount of carbon emissions each of us is personally responsible for is known as our carbon footprint.

Personal sources of carbon dioxide include fuel burned for heating and cooking, and fuels used in car engines and other forms of transport. It also includes fuels burned in electricity-generating stations to produce the electricity you use, and the carbon dioxide emitted in the production and transport of the food you eat and the things you buy.

On average, each person in the world is responsible for putting four tonnes of carbon dioxide into the atmosphere each year. Your own carbon footprint depends on your lifestyle, and this depends mainly on where you live in the world. People in Western countries have much larger carbon footprints than people in less economically developed countries. For example, a typical US citizen has a carbon footprint of 20 tonnes, and a typical Ethiopian has a carbon footprint of just 0.1 tonnes.

## The national picture

So which countries have the largest carbon footprints? It's the traditional industrial nations, such as the United States, the UK and Japan, and also newly industrialized countries such as China and India. China and the United States lead the way, each

## CASE STUDY

### THE BLAME GAME

China and India are growing fast as industrial nations, and their carbon emissions are also growing fast as a result. They are criticized by other nations, but argue that each Chinese or Indian citizen has a much lower carbon footprint than a typical American or European. They also argue that they have a right to industrialize, as other nations have before them. After all, the United States is responsible for a third of all the carbon dioxide emissions in history, and 20 per cent of annual emissions, despite having just 5 per cent of the world's population.

of them producing about 20 per cent of all carbon emissions.

## The overall picture

There are about 3,000 gigatonnes of carbon dioxide in the atmosphere. Every year we are adding about 26 gigatonnes to this amount, a figure that is gradually rising as the world's population increases and people's standard of living improves. This is shown by the Keeling Curve (see page 12) getting steeper and steeper.

Once carbon dioxide is in the atmosphere, its effects are the same no matter who was responsible for it. It's unfortunate that some people with very low carbon footprints could be the most badly affected by global warming.

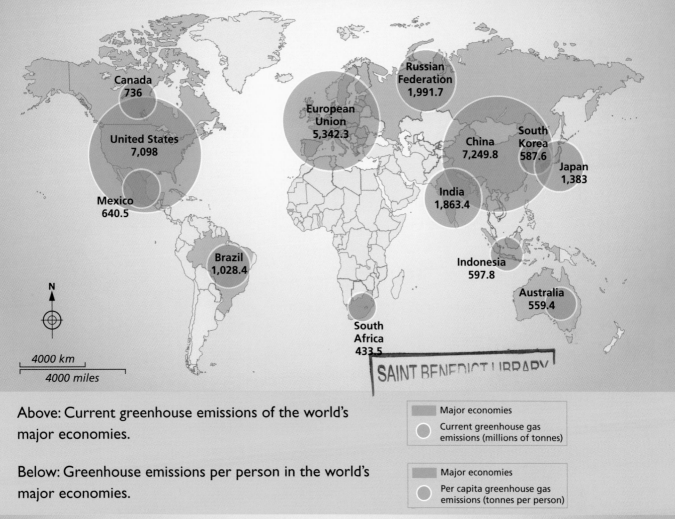

Above: Current greenhouse emissions of the world's major economies.

Below: Greenhouse emissions per person in the world's major economies.

| | |
|---|---|
| Major economies | |
| Current greenhouse gas emissions (millions of tonnes) | |

| | |
|---|---|
| Major economies | |
| Per capita greenhouse gas emissions (tonnes per person) | |

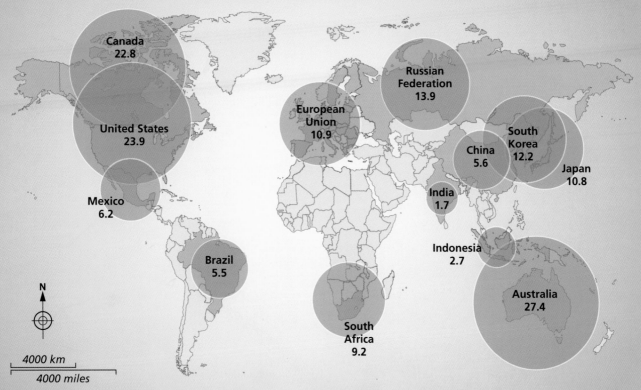

# 4: Evidence for Global Warming

How do we know that global warming is actually happening? We have two types of evidence: measurements of what's happening in the atmosphere and oceans (such as air temperature and sea temperature), and observable evidence – that is, evidence we can see with our own eyes.

## Weather and climate records

There is a huge network of weather stations across the world. Each day, often several times a day, instruments (for example, thermometers, barometers and anemometers) record all aspects of the weather, including air temperature, air pressure, wind direction and speed, rainfall and hours of sunshine. Measurements are also taken by instruments sent up into the atmosphere on weather balloons, and by remote sensing from satellites.

All this data is used in weather forecasting. It is also stored so that changes in climate can be tracked over time. Accurate records have been kept in many locations for more than a hundred years, and comparisons show that the average air temperature is rising.

Weather records are stored by national weather organizations, such as the National Oceanic and Atmospheric Administration (NOAA) in the United States and the Meteorological Office in the UK. These organizations share data, often through the World Meteorological Organization.

The oceans play a huge role in global warming, so they are measured, too. Data collected includes water temperature at the surface and different depths, the strength of ocean currents and the amount of carbon dioxide dissolved in the water.

## Adjusting the figures

Comparing weather records from different years is not always straightforward. There are many factors that affect the climate, and these must be taken into account when assessing whether a rise in greenhouse gases can be linked to global warming. For example, in the early 1990s the world cooled slightly because of ash in the atmosphere from the eruption of Mount Pinatubo in the Philippines.

## Observable evidence

Some of the changes caused by global warming are visible and observable. They include retreating glaciers, a reduction in sea ice and rising sea levels. There's more on all these changes in later chapters. Some of the changes are observed on the ground; others are observed remotely from satellites. For example, the Global Land Ice Measurements from Space (GLIMS) project uses satellite photography to monitor how glaciers are shrinking. Sea levels are measured to the nearest millimetre using radar altimeters on satellites.

The reduction in Arctic sea ice is observable evidence of global warming.

— Average extent of sea ice, 1979–83
— Average extent of sea ice, 2002–6
☐ Minimum extent of sea ice, 2007

Arctic Circle

RUSSIA

Alaska (USA)

North pole

NORWAY

GREENLAND

CANADA

500 km
500 miles

These canisters contain ice cores drilled from the enormously thick Greenland ice sheet. They are stored in a vast freezer. The cores will be examined to determine the levels of carbon dioxide in the atmosphere thousands of years ago.

## Long-term climate change

Global warming is nothing new. In the long history of our planet, global temperatures have regularly risen, creating periods a few degrees warmer than today. These have alternated with periods of global cooling, when temperatures were a few degrees colder than today. So in the long term, over millions of years, climate change is natural.

At the moment the Earth is in the middle of a long, cool period. Temperatures slowly began to drop about 2.7 million years ago. Since then there have been very cold periods, known as ice ages, with less cold 'interglacial periods' between them. During the ice ages, much of the northern hemisphere was covered by a layer of ice more than a kilometre thick. The last ice age ended just 12,000 years ago, after lasting for 100,000 years.

## Long-term evidence

How do we know what the Earth's climate was like millions of years ago? The clues come from materials trapped in rocks and ice at the time. Fossils found in rocks show what sort of animals and plants lived in a place in the past, and these are a clue to the climate of the time. The growth rings in fossilized trees show how good growing conditions were.

Ancient ice in the world's ice sheets contains bubbles of air up to a million years old. Bubbles from ice cores drilled from Antarctica and Greenland are used to find the levels of different gases in the

atmosphere in the distant past. Historical documents provide clues to more recent changes in climate. For example, written records and paintings tell us that the climate was cooler in northern Europe between about 1300 and 1850, a period now known as the Little Ice Age.

## Causes of long-term climate change

Long-term climate changes are caused mainly by variations in the Earth's movement around the Sun, and the Sun itself. The angle of tilt of the Earth's axis alters slightly over thousands of years, and the axis also moves slowly around so that the Earth is like a wobbly spinning top. The shape of the Earth's orbit also slowly changes, moving it closer to, or further from, the Sun. The heat output of the Sun also varies. All these factors mean that the amount of heat reaching different parts of the Earth slowly changes over thousands of years in long cycles.

# 5: Global Warming and the Weather

Global warming is causing temperatures to rise, but its effects aren't limited to that. We are also experiencing other changes to our climate, including a shift in rainfall patterns and an increase in extreme weather events, such as hurricanes and snowstorms. All these changes are having a major impact on the natural world.

## Temperature changes

Every year, three different organizations – the NOAA and NASA (National Aeronautics and Space Administration) in the United States, and the Meteorological Office in the UK – work out an average global temperature from the millions of weather records taken over the previous year. For the year 2008–9, they all came up with a figure of about 14.5°C.

To assess how global temperatures are changing, temperature measurements are normally compared to the average temperature during the period 1961–90. That was 14°C, so the average global temperature is now 0.5°C higher than it was then. Compared to the beginning of the twentieth century, it is 0.8°C higher.

The average global temperature is an average across the whole globe – the average temperature in some places is much higher and in other places it is much lower. Likewise, the rise of 0.5°C since the 1961–90 period is also an average. In some places

the rise has been several degrees; in others the temperature has even dropped a little (see map on page 13).

## Changing rainfall patterns

Rainfall patterns are beginning to change across the globe, too. Scientists have

(see map on page 13).

## CASE STUDY

### DROUGHT IN SOUTH-WEST AUSTRALIA

Levels of rainfall have fallen slowly across south-west Australia for more than half a century. In the 1970s they fell quite quickly. Today, the area gets only about 85 per cent of the rain that it used to get. This long-term trend is blamed partly on global warming (it may also be linked to changes in large-scale air currents over the continent and land-use change in Australia). It has caused drought conditions in the area for many decades. The city of Perth has opened a desalination plant to supplement the water supply.

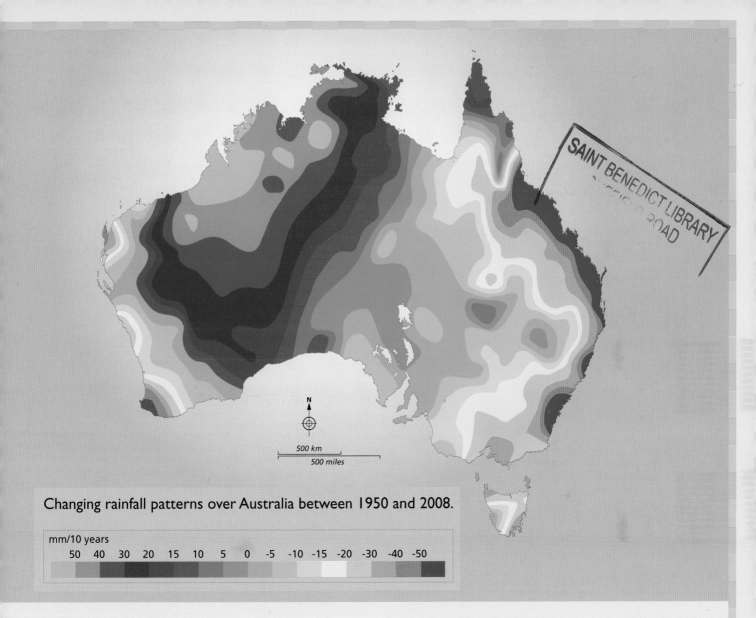

Changing rainfall patterns over Australia between 1950 and 2008.

mm/10 years

| 50 | 40 | 30 | 20 | 15 | 10 | 5 | 0 | -5 | -10 | -15 | -20 | -30 | -40 | -50 |

calculated that the land area of the Earth is getting about 1 per cent more rain than it was 100 years ago. This is probably because higher air and ocean temperatures are allowing more water vapour to evaporate into the atmosphere.

The change is uneven: some places have experienced a rise in annual rainfall while in other places it has fallen. For example, in the eastern parts of North America and South America and northern Europe and Asia, there is 5 per cent more rain falling than 100 years ago; however, in the Mediterranean, southern Africa and southern Asia, declining levels of rainfall are a problem.

As well as these changes in annual rainfall patterns, there are also changes in the frequency and heaviness of rainfall. These can be just as problematic. In some places, rain is falling more heavily, but less frequently, leading to periods of flood, followed by periods of drought.

## Extreme events

Non-experts often blame extreme weather events, such as powerful hurricanes, snow storms, heat waves and very cold conditions, on global warming. There is certainly evidence that some types of extreme weather events are becoming more frequent and more intense. In 2009 alone, extreme events included Hurricane Rick, the second most powerful hurricane on record in the eastern Pacific, heavy rains in Brazil that caused floods and mudslides, and record snowfalls across the north-eastern United States. However, we cannot say for sure that any of these events were the direct result of global warming, or that they prove that climate change is happening.

## Tropical cyclones

Tropical cyclones are vast, spinning storms that form over the tropics. They have different names in different parts of the world. In the Americas they are called hurricanes; in South-East Asia they are known as typhoons. Tropical cyclones get their energy from warm tropical oceans, so warming oceans are likely to cause more intense tropical cyclones.

These storms bring damaging winds and flooding when they hit land. The number of very intense hurricanes in the North Atlantic has increased, even though the overall number of hurricanes each year has not. The year 2005 was a good example. Three of the six most powerful hurricanes ever recorded hit the United States. They included Hurricane Katrina, which caused devastating floods in New Orleans. In the same year, on the other side of world, a record three cyclones hit Australia. More powerful storms are a real threat to low-lying coasts, especially when combined with rising sea levels (see pages 34–35).

Storms that form away from the tropics are less powerful than tropical cyclones, but can still bring damaging winds and sometimes coastal flooding. Evidence shows that these storms are forming further towards the Earth's poles, and that they are getting more powerful, although less frequent.

## Heat waves

A heat wave is an extended period when summer temperatures are well above normal. Heat waves are dangerous because the public and the authorities are not used to coping with extreme temperatures. They have become more common over the land areas of the globe. When a heat wave hit Europe in August 2003, the temperature in France soared to 35°C for nine days running. More than 13,000 people died from the effects. Many climate scientists link this heat wave to global warming. As global warming continues, heat waves are likely to become more common.

# PERSPECTIVES

## HURRICANE KATRINA

There was much debate about whether Hurricane Katrina was caused by global warming. It is possible that it was, but there is no proof. However, the event was seen by many as a wake-up call for the United States and the world. Former US vice president Al Gore said:

*What changed in the United States with Hurricane Katrina was a feeling that we have entered a period of consequences.*

Devastation in New Orleans following Hurricane Katrina.

## Changes for plants and animals

Rising temperatures, changing rainfall patterns and the increase in extreme weather events are affecting plants and animals, and these effects will become more pronounced as global warming continues.

In general, changes that take place in spring are happening a little earlier. These events include greening (when fresh plant growth appears after the winter), migrations (birds and other animals moving to their spring and summer homes), and egg-laying by birds. The length of the growing season for plants is also increasing.

Plants and animals are adapted to live in certain climates. As climates change, some species can spread to new areas – some plant and animal species that are adapted to warm climates are spreading north and south towards the poles as conditions become more favourable to them. Butterflies are very sensitive to temperature changes and so are good indicators of global warming. In Europe, some butterfly species are no longer found in their original habitats because temperatures have grown too warm for them. They now live further north. In North America, forest trees are dying because of warmer winters and because of damage from certain species of beetles, which are spreading north because of milder temperatures.

Drier, hotter conditions created in some places by global warming make forest fires more likely.

## Crop problems

Like other plants, crops are affected by changes in temperature and rainfall. The effects are favourable in some areas – in northern Europe plants are less affected by cold weather and frosts, and farmers will be able to grow crops for more time each year. But in the tropics, where the majority of the world's food is grown, some traditional crops may become impossible to grow, perhaps because it's too hot or too dry. This could create food shortages in some poorer areas of the world. However, in the next few decades, unless temperatures soar too high, the area of the world's surface suitable for growing crops is expected to increase. It's also possible that rising carbon dioxide levels will help plant growth.

As global warming continues, some species face extinction unless they can adapt to new conditions. One study predicts that a quarter of species in some areas will die off.

## Habitat changes

Temperature rises have also been affecting the habitats where plants and animals live. Deserts and forests have been shifting positions. The edges of some deserts are moving towards the poles, taking over grasslands as they go. And plants are spreading to higher altitudes. The tree line in Russia's Ural Mountains is now 80 metres higher than it was a century ago.

## CASE STUDY

### MALARIA IN AFRICA

Over the last 40 years, malaria-carrying mosquitoes have been spreading the disease to the highland areas of East Africa. The spread is being partly blamed on global warming, as higher temperatures are allowing mosquitoes to survive in places that would have been too cold for them in earlier periods. The same is true in highland areas of Indonesia and Afghanistan, and malaria has even spread to parts of Italy.

# 6: Global Warming and Ice

It's no surprise that as the world warms up, some of its ice melts away. It's the most visible effect of global warming so far. As temperatures at the Earth's poles and on its mountain ranges gradually rise, glaciers (slowly moving rivers of ice), ice caps (thick sheets of ice) and sea ice (ice formed when the sea freezes) all start to shrink.

## The Arctic

The centre of the Arctic Ocean is permanently frozen, forming a thick layer of sea ice. As the temperature drops each winter, more sea freezes, so the area of ice increases, reaching some of the land that surrounds the Arctic Ocean. In the warmer summer, the ice retreats towards the Pole.

In the last 40 years, the area of Arctic sea ice has reduced by about 20 per cent. The ice is also getting thinner. It is predicted that by 2030 there will be no sea ice in the Arctic in the summer. Coasts that were once protected by ice in winter are now being eroded by storms, and low-lying islands, coastal villages and towns are all threatened by floods. Local people are unable to hunt seals on the ice as they once did. The same is true for polar bears, which hunt seals in spring. Loss of ice has reduced their hunting season, leaving them hungry and forcing them to hunt on land and scavenge for food around towns and villages. Another victim is the ringed seal, which brings up its young on the Arctic ice.

## The Antarctic

The Antarctic continent is covered by a thick ice cap that contains two-thirds of the world's fresh water. Although the centre of the ice sheet is still getting thicker, some of the sea ice around the edge of the continent is breaking up.

## Glaciers and ice caps

The world's glaciers and ice caps are shrinking, too. In the Alps, for example, a

## FACTS and FIGURES

### ARCTIC TEMPERATURES

The Arctic (the region around the North Pole) has already suffered a dramatic increase in temperatures due to global warming. It is around 4°C warmer in winter than it was 50 years ago (compared to an average global warming of less than 1°C).

third of the total area of glaciers has gone. Greenland is the largest island in the world and almost completely covered in an ice cap more than 2 kilometres thick. The ice cap formed from snowfalls over hundreds of millions of years. The glaciers that flow down from the Greenland ice cap are melting back. One of the largest reduced in length by 5 kilometres in 2005 alone.

Ice falling from the end of the Perito Moreno Glacier in Patagonia, Argentina. Glaciers lose ice like this each summer, but global warming is accelerating the process, so that the ends of glaciers are retreating in many parts of the world.

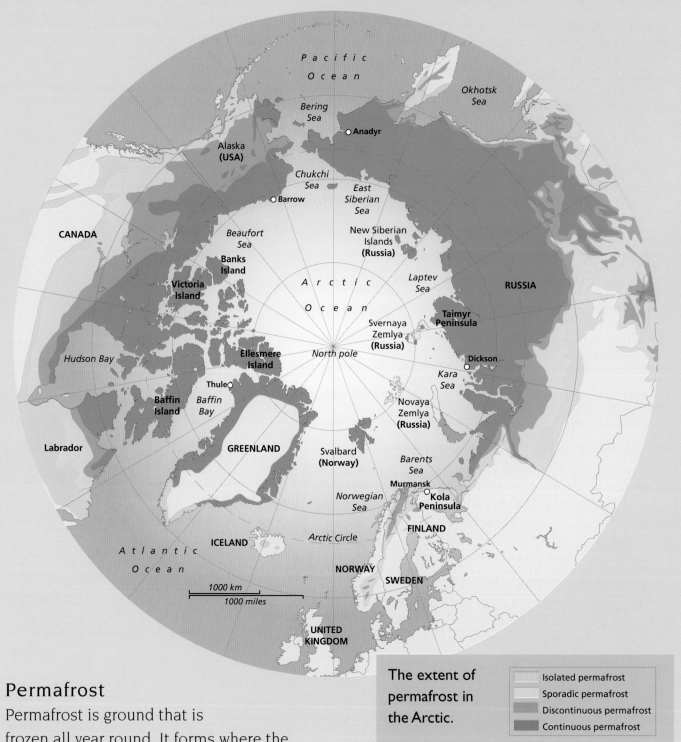

The extent of permafrost in the Arctic.

| | |
|---|---|
| | Isolated permafrost |
| | Sporadic permafrost |
| | Discontinuous permafrost |
| | Continuous permafrost |

# Permafrost

Permafrost is ground that is frozen all year round. It forms where the average annual temperature is below freezing. There is permafrost in the Arctic, around the Arctic and in Antarctica. In all, about a fifth of the Earth's land area, including half of Canada and Russia is permafrost. It has existed for hundreds of thousands of years. Permafrost is as hard as concrete and, in places, hundreds of metres deep. In places where summer temperatures

**MARY SIMON**

Mary Simon is president of the Inuit people. Speaking in 2009 about climate change in the Arctic, she said:

*My message is that climate change is not abstract; it is about people's lives. The contamination of food sources, the breaking up of Inuit houses as the Arctic permafrost melts, the disruption of the traditional rhythms of Inuit life – these are some of the ways that climate change is affecting the community.*

rise above freezing, the top layer of the permafrost thaws for part of the year.

There is evidence that the permafrost is thawing because of global warming. Since 1990, the area of permafrost where the surface remains frozen in summer has reduced by about 7 per cent. In areas where the surface does thaw, the thaw is penetrating deeper. The loss of permafrost is not given as much publicity as melting sea ice and glaciers, perhaps because it's not so visible. But its consequences may be just as serious.

## Effects of thawing permafrost

Loss of permafrost changes the nature of the ground, which affects the plants, animals and people who live on it. When the ground thaws, the water formed in the ground drains away, and the ground collapses slightly. Trees topple as their roots are left in soft soil. Buildings built on permafrost crack as their foundations move. The city of Fairbanks, Alaska, for example, has been badly affected by thawing permafrost. Thawing permafrost also leads to landslides and lake formation. Changing ground conditions mean that animals such as reindeer (caribou) cannot migrate and feed as before, and birds and mammals lose their habitats (although the thawed ground provides a habitat for new species to become established).

## Methane from permafrost

There are billions of tonnes of substances called methane hydrates locked in permafrost. A methane hydrate is made up of methane attached to water. Experts are concerned that if the thaw of the world's permafrost continues, large amounts of methane will be released from the water and move into the atmosphere. Methane is a greenhouse gas with high heat-trapping capabilities. So, as the permafrost melts because of global warming, the release of methane could further accelerate the greenhouse effect. In the worst-case scenario – that is, if all the permafrost melts – the effects of this methane could outstrip the effects of all the carbon dioxide we've ever released into the atmosphere.

# 7: Global Warming and the Oceans

The oceans, which cover two-thirds of the Earth's surface, are being affected by global warming in many ways. The most well-known change is the rise in sea levels, but there are others, too. The temperature of the oceans is rising, and so is the amount of carbon dioxide they contain. All these changes are having knock-on effects on the land, on weather patterns, on the plants and animals that live in and around the oceans, and on people living in coastal areas.

## Warming waters

The oceans interact closely with the Earth's atmosphere. Heat energy passes between the atmosphere and the oceans so that sometimes the atmosphere warms the oceans, and sometimes the oceans warm the atmosphere. The oceans have taken up more than 10 per cent of the heat added to the Earth by global warming, and warming has reached depths of 3,000 metres or more. The overall increase in the surface temperature in the last 50 years is about 0.3°C. That doesn't sound much, but it is significant. The higher temperature means that the water has expanded a little, pushing up sea levels by a few centimetres. (Sea levels are also rising because of melting glaciers and ice caps – see pages 34–35.) Water also evaporates more quickly from warm seas, adding extra water vapour to the atmosphere.

## Effects on animals and plants

Just as changes in air temperature are a threat to plants and animals on land, increasing sea and ocean temperatures are a threat to marine plants and animals. The ranges of marine animals (the areas where they live) will alter and the numbers of fish in oceans near the poles will change.

## FACTS and FIGURES

### EFFECTS OF WARMING ON CORAL REEFS

Warming is affecting the world's coral reefs. Corals are formed by animals called polyps. Their beautiful colours are made by microscopic plants called algae that live in the polyps. When the water warms by just a degree or so, the delicate balance between the polyps and their algae is upset. The algae die and the reefs lose their colour.

A coral reef in a tropical sea. The white patch is bleached coral, caused by a slight rise in water temperature.

Marine animals will migrate at different times. Already, some species, such as the leatherback turtle, are seen in seas further north than before.

Plankton are tiny marine animals and plants. There are countless billions of them in the oceans. Many species of plankton live in cold water and can be killed off if the water warms up even slightly. Any loss of plankton can lead to a collapse in populations of other species, as plankton are at the bottom of the ocean's food chain.

## Changing patterns

The oceans have currents that move through them, circulating warm and cool water. These currents are not constant, but go through cycles of change (flowing more slowly at certain times of year, for example). Rising ocean water temperatures, together with changing wind patterns, are likely to disrupt the currents and their cycles.

For example, the system of ocean currents in the North Atlantic could be affected. One current in this system, the Gulf Stream, brings warm water to the seas around northern Europe. As a result, the winters there are milder than other places at the same latitude. If the Gulf Stream is disrupted, it may mean cooler winters.

The El Niño–Southern Oscillation (ENSO) is a movement of water and air, in the form of currents and winds, across the southern Pacific. During an El Niño event, the normal pattern of winds and currents is changed, bringing different weather to areas on each side of the Pacific, such as droughts to Australia. This is one of many similar cycles that are likely to be affected by changing ocean temperatures. We don't yet know exactly how they will be affected, because we still have a lot to learn about how these cycles work.

## FACTS and FIGURES

### THE OCEAN AS A CARBON SINK

Every year we add an amazing 26 gigatonnes of carbon dioxide to the atmosphere through carbon dioxide emissions and deforestation. But each year the oceans soak up about seven of those gigatonnes of carbon dioxide (about a quarter of the total). The carbon dioxide becomes dissolved in the water.

## Rising sea levels

One of the most worrying consequences of global warming is rising sea levels. This is happening because water is flowing into the oceans from melting glaciers and ice caps, and because the ocean water is expanding slightly as its temperature rises. Just over half of the sea level rises caused by global warming have come from expansion, and the rest from melting glaciers and ice caps (the melting of sea ice makes no difference

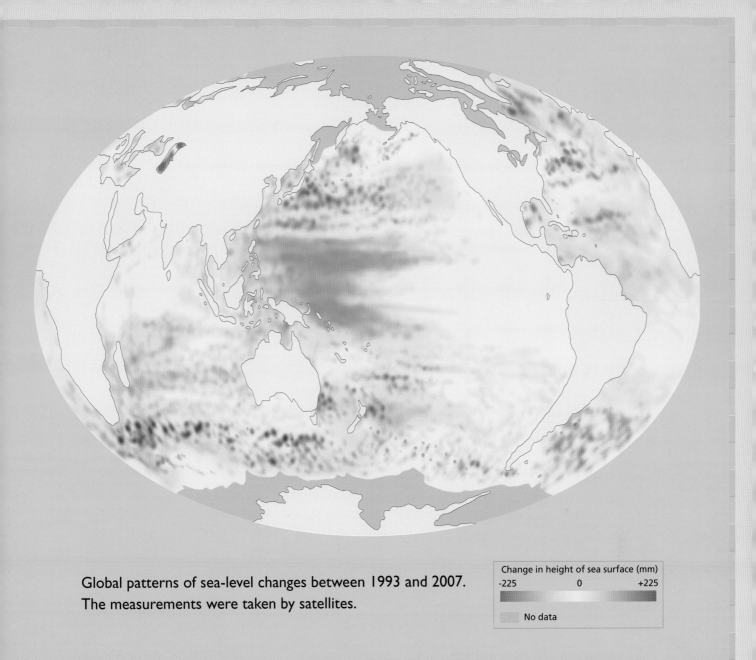

Global patterns of sea-level changes between 1993 and 2007.
The measurements were taken by satellites.

Change in height of sea surface (mm)

-225    0    +225

No data

to sea levels because the ice is floating in the sea anyway). Sea level rises happen all over the globe, not just where water is added to the oceans.

Global sea levels have gone up and down many times as climates have changed during Earth's history. Sea levels fall when the world cools and water becomes locked up in ice caps. They rise when the world warms up and the ice caps melt. There are no accurate historical records of sea levels, so it's difficult to measure the changes exactly. However, scientists estimate that sea levels have risen by between 10 and 25 cm over the last century, and that the current rate of sea level rise is about 3 millimetres per year.

One of the hundreds of beautiful islands that make up the Maldives in the Indian Ocean. This island would disappear if the sea level rose by just one metre.

## Sea-level predictions

So how much will sea levels rise in the future? Answering this question depends on many factors – how much more carbon dioxide we put into the atmosphere each year; how far temperatures rise; and how much of the ice caps melt – and many of these things are uncertain. That's why a range of figures is given. In the 2007, the IPCC estimated that sea levels would rise by 18 to 59 centimetres by the year 2100. However, other studies give higher figures, with worse-case scenarios of up to 2 metres.

What happens in the longer-term future is very uncertain. However, if the Greenland ice cap melted completely (which is a possibility in a few hundred years time if Arctic temperatures rise by another 2°C), then enough water would flow into the sea to raise sea levels by 7 metres. An even greater catastrophe would occur if the whole of the Western Antarctic ice sheet melted.

## CASE STUDY

### THE MALDIVES

The Maldives are a group of coral islands in the Indian Ocean. There are 1,190 islands in all, but only 202 are inhabited by the country's population of 270,000. The average elevation of the Maldives is just 1 metre, so the islands are at risk from sea-level rises. According to current predictions, the islands could mostly disappear under the waves by the year 2100.

There's no suggestion at the moment that global warming will become severe enough to cause this, but if it did, sea levels would rise by a staggering 60 metres.

## Problems of sea-level rises

The most obvious effect of sea-level rises is that low-lying coastal land and low-lying islands will be flooded by the sea. Sea-level rises will also leave coastal areas more prone to temporary flooding from storm surges during hurricanes and other storms (which may become more intense with global warming). Coastal erosion will also become more severe.

The current rise in sea levels is already causing more floods during high tides. Venice is a famous example, where a combination of subsidence and rising sea levels means that the city's squares are under water for roughly 200 days a year.

As sea levels continue to rise, coastal floods will probably become more frequent. The areas likely to be affected first by these floods are the world's major deltas (a delta is the low-lying land created by sediment deposited in the sea at the mouth of a river). They include densely populated regions such as southern Bangladesh, the Mississippi delta and the Nile delta.

Many of the world's major cities, including London, New York, Bangkok and Tokyo, are built on land just a few metres above sea level. Major sea level rises could lead to frequent flooding and potential disaster for these cities.

# 8: The Way Ahead

The previous chapters have discussed what global warming is, what its effects are and how it is threatening the planet, plants and animals, and us. Climates are changing and many plants and animals are being forced to find new habitats, or face extinction. Scientists have estimated that 160,000 people die each year from the effects of climate change.

We must try to slow, stop and then reverse global warming. That means reducing carbon emissions as fast as possible. It's a simple idea, but it must be balanced with the need to keep the world's economy running, which currently relies on the use of fossil fuels. In the meantime, we must prepare for the effects of global warming.

## A history of climate research

We know today that human-made global warming began more than 200 years ago, as the Industrial Revolution got under way. But it was not until the 1890s that a link was suggested (by Swedish chemist Svante Arrhenius) between the level of carbon dioxide in the atmosphere and the Earth's temperature. In the 1930s it was suggested that carbon dioxide from burning fuels could be responsible for rising temperatures. Accurate measurements of carbon dioxide levels began in the 1950s, and over the years the increase in levels was charted.

Climate models were first developed in the 1960s. A climate model is a computer program that works out what will happen to the atmosphere, oceans and ice caps in the future. As climatologists understand more

## PERSPECTIVES

**THREATS TO TUVALU**

Tuvalu is a group of islands in the Pacific Ocean. The islands are coral atolls and lie just one or two metres above sea level. In 2003, in a speech to the United Nations, Saufatu Sopoanga, Prime Minister of Tuvalu, criticized the main carbon-emitting nations:

*We live in constant fear of the adverse impacts of climate change. For a coral atoll nation, sea level rise and more severe weather events loom as a growing threat to our entire population. The threat is real and serious, and is of no difference to a slow and insidious form of terrorism against us.*

about how the atmosphere works, climate models are becoming more accurate.

In the 1970s, scientists made a positive link between rising carbon dioxide levels and global warming. Environmental campaigners began to publicize the problem, although at the time temperatures were cooling slightly. Temperatures began rising again in the 1980s, but there was little response from governments. In 1988 the United States suffered a country-wide drought and record temperatures. That year, a NASA scientist named James Hanson told the US Congress that he was 99 per cent sure global warming was happening as a result of human-made carbon emissions. Governments around the world finally began to take notice.

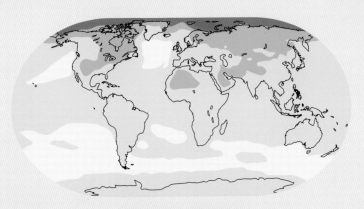

**2011–2030**

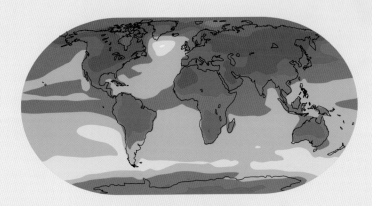

**2046–2065**

These maps show probable future global temperature rises caused by global warming. They assume we manage to considerably reduce carbon emissions.

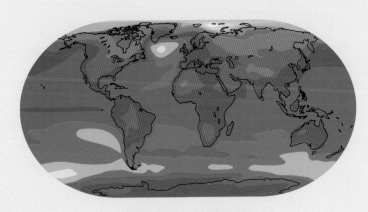

**2080–2099**

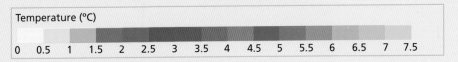

Temperature (ºC)

0   0.5   1   1.5   2   2.5   3   3.5   4   4.5   5   5.5   6   6.5   7   7.5

## The IPCC and climate conferences

In 1989 the Intergovernmental Panel on Climate Change (IPCC) was formed so that scientists from different countries could work together on the challenge of global warming. Its first assessment on the state of the climate was published in 1990, and it has published further reports every few years since then. In 1992 government representatives met at the Earth Summit in Rio de Janeiro, Brazil, to discuss global warming and to begin negotiating a response to it. At Rio an agreement known as the United Nations Framework Convention on Climate Change (UNFCCC) was signed by 16 countries.

Years of negotiations followed in an attempt to agree which countries should cut their carbon emissions and by how much. Emissions targets for each country were finally agreed at a summit in Kyoto, Japan, in 1997. Most countries signed up to the Kyoto Protocol, which is now international law. Under its terms, some countries were allowed to keep their emissions stable, and some were allowed to increase them.

Negotiations for a successor to the Kyoto Protocol have not gone smoothly. At the Copenhagen summit in December 2009, there was conflict over emissions targets between the United States and the European Union on one side, and newly industrialized nations such as China and Brazil on the other. Some countries signed an agreement called the Copenhagen Accord, but the emissions targets agreed to were voluntary and not legally binding. A target of keeping global warming to no more than 2°C above pre-industrial levels now looks likely to fail. However, the world's richer countries did agree to help developing countries develop low-carbon technologies in the future.

## The sceptics

Today, most scientists agree that global warming is happening and is being driven mainly by human-made emissions of greenhouse gases. However, some people do not accept this view of the situation. These climate-change sceptics, scientists among them, are not convinced by the

## CASE STUDY

### CLIMATEGATE

In November 2009, emails exchanged by climate scientists in the UK were leaked to the press. Climate-change sceptics alleged that the emails contained evidence that the scientists had fiddled with data to make it look as though climate change is worse than it really is. According to the sceptics, the emails showed that scientific evidence against climate change had been hidden. Subsequent investigations found that the scientists were innocent of the allegations, but public trust in climate science was damaged.

Stop **CLIMATE CHANGE** Here

GREENPEACE

BLA BLA

CLIMATE JUSTICE

A BLA

NOW!

ge The Futur

GREENPEACE

THERE IS NO PLANET B

NATURE DOESN'T MPROMISE

MONSIEU
PRES/DE

T NOW!

IMATE
YOUR
PAN

BLA BLA BLA...

ACT NO

CHA
THE
POLIT
NOT TH
CLIMATE

THERE IS NO PLANET B

NATURE DOESN'T COMPROMISE

ders Act

Environmental campaigners at the Climate Summit in Copenhagen, Denmark, in December 2009. Tens of thousands took part in marches to advertise the dangers of global warming.

evidence for global warming, and they deny that global warming is a human-made problem. They argue that current global warming is part of a natural cycle, that climate data is wrong, that computer models are flawed, and that being a bit warmer will be beneficial anyway. In the 1990s, oil companies and motor manufacturers sided with the sceptics because they were concerned that cuts in the use of fuel to reduce carbon emissions would lead to loss of trade. At the same time, some government-funded climate scientists in the United States claimed they were prevented by government officials from revealing their evidence for climate change.

## Climate change mitigation

Climate change mitigation means trying to slow, stop or even reverse global warming. The most obvious method of mitigation is to reduce carbon dioxide emissions so that the amount of carbon dioxide in the atmosphere stops rising. The longer we do nothing, the harder it will be to recover the situation. It is estimated that we will have to cut emissions drastically, perhaps by 50 per cent by the year 2050, to avoid temperatures rising by more than another 1°C by the end of the century.

## Reducing emissions

The main way to reduce carbon emissions is to reduce fossil fuel use. This means using less energy all around, including electricity, because most electricity is produced by burning fossil fuels. At home, you can switch things off, use appliances for less time, use energy-efficient appliances and light bulbs, and make sure your home is insulated. Away from home, you can try to travel less by car and plane, try to buy only things that have a low carbon footprint, and buy carbon offsets (these pay for carbon-reducing schemes around the world).

On a larger scale, we need to change the methods we use to generate electricity, by switching as much as possible to renewable sources such as solar and wind power, and possibly also to nuclear energy (although this has its own environmental problems, and is banned in some countries).

## Catching carbon

Carbon capture and storage (also called sequestration) is a new technology that is currently being tested. It removes carbon dioxide from power station emissions before it goes into the atmosphere. The carbon is stored where it can do no harm (in future this is likely to be in old oil and gas wells). Carbon capture will allow us to carry on using fossil fuels in power stations without adding carbon dioxide to the atmosphere.

## Adaptation

Like thousands of species of plants and animals have done before us, we may have to adapt to survive the effects of global warming. That means, for example, developing crops that will grow in changed climates, providing better warnings of extreme weather events, abandoning flooded land, and even moving whole cities if sea levels rise by several metres.

## Conclusion

In reality, we must both mitigate to reduce global warming and adapt to its effects. If we don't take action now to stop global warming, it will be hard for us to adapt fast enough to avoid catastrophe.

Environmentalists plant trees in Costa Rica to try to repair some of the damage to the rainforest, and so help to slow global warming.

## A LONG-TERM PROBLEM

If we can stop global warming in its tracks, it will still take a long time for the Earth to recover. According to the IPCC assessment report of 2007:

*Both past and future anthropogenic $CO_2$ emissions will continue to contribute to warming and sea-level rise for more than a millennium, due to the time scales required for the removal of this gas from the atmosphere.*

# Glossary

**anthropogenic** Describes anything that comes from human activities – for example, the carbon dioxide from burning fuels is anthropogenic.

**carbon dioxide** A gas consisting of carbon and oxygen that is found naturally in the atmosphere, but also formed when fuels are burned.

**carbon emission** Any carbon dioxide that is emitted into the atmosphere by burning fossil fuels.

**carbon sink** A part of the Earth that absorbs carbon dioxide from the atmosphere. The oceans and the rainforests are carbon sinks.

**CFCs** Chlorofluorocarbons (CFCs) are a type of gas emitted by fridges and aerosols that harm the ozone layer in the Earth's atmosphere.

**climate change** Changes in the world's climates, probably caused by human carbon dioxide emissions.

**climatologist** A scientist who studies climates and how they are changing.

**desalination** Removing salt from sea water to make fresh water.

**fossil fuels** Coal, oil and gas, which are formed from the remains of ancient plants and animals.

**gigatonne** A thousand, million tonnes.

**glacier** A body of ice that moves gradually downhill from an ice cap, like a slow-moving frozen river.

**global warming** The gradual increase in the average temperature of the Earth's atmosphere, probably caused by human carbon dioxide emissions.

**greenhouse effect** The process that traps heat from the Sun in the Earth's atmosphere.

**greenhouse gas** Any of the gases in the atmosphere (mainly carbon dioxide, methane and water vapour) that are responsible for the greenhouse effect.

**growing season** The part of the year (spring and summer) when plants make new growth.

**growth ring** One of a series of concentric rings of wood seen when a tree trunk or branch is cut into sections. Each ring is the growth of wood for a year, and the thickness of each ring shows how good the climate was for growing that year.

**habitat** A place where animals and plants live.

**ice age** One of a number of periods in history when temperatures were cooler than today and thick ice sheets covered much of the northern hemisphere.

**ice cap** A thick layer of ice that covers the top of a mountain range or land in polar regions.

**Industrial Revolution** The period beginning in the second half of the 18th century when Britain, Europe and the United States experienced a surge in productivity and wealth due to the widespread adoption of large-scale, mechanical means of production.

**IPCC** International Panel on Climate Change: a United Nations organization that reports on climate change.

**low-carbon technology** Any technology that reduces carbon emissions.

**malaria** Infectious disease that is often fatal, caused by microorganisms in the blood, and spread by mosquitoes that suck blood from the skin.

**meteorologist** A scientist who studies the weather.

**methane** A gas made up of carbon and hydrogen that is a powerful greenhouse gas.

**NASA** National Aeronautics and Space Administration: A US government organization responsible for space exploration and aeronautics and aerospace research.

**NOAA** National Oceanic and Atmospheric Administration: a US government organization that observes the oceans and atmosphere.

**permafrost** Ground that is frozen solid all year round.

**photosynthesis** The process by which plants use sunlight to make food from carbon dioxide and water.

**remote sensing** Gathering data about an object from a distance, without being in contact with the object (for example, measuring the temperature of the atmosphere from satellites in space).

**sceptic** A person who does not believe in a particular idea or theory.

**sediment** Particles of rock made by erosion and carried down a river by the current.

**storm surge** A rise in sea level under a large storm, caused by the low air pressure inside the storm.

**water vapour** The gaseous form of water, made when water evaporates.

**weather balloon** A large balloon that carries measuring instruments up into the atmosphere to record things like air temperature and air pressure.

# Further Information

## Books

*Can the Earth Cope? Climate Change* by Richard Spilsbury (Wayland, 2008)

*Eyewitness: Climate Change* (Dorling Kindersley, 2008)

*Groundworks series: Climate Change* by Shelley Tanaka (A&C Black, 2010)

*Science at the Edge: Global Warming* by Sally Morgan (Raintree, 2009)

*Science in the News: Climate Change* by Chris Oxlade (Watts, 2008)

## Websites

www.foe.co.uk/campaigns/climate_change.html
Friends of the Earth campaign to fight climate change.

www.ipcc.ch
Website of the Intergovernmental Panel on Climate Change.

www.metoffice.gov.uk/climatechange/
Information about climate change from the UK's Meteorological Office.

nsidc.org/frozenground/
Information on permafrost from the US National Snow and Ice Data Center.

www.research.noaa.gov/climate/
Information on climate change from the US National Oceanic and Atmospheric Administration

# Index

Page numbers in **bold** refer to maps and photos.